almost home

also by madisen kuhn

please don't go before i get better

eighteen years

Almost Home

Madisen Kuhn

GALLERY BOOKS

New York   London   Toronto   Sydney   New Delhi

G

Gallery Books
An Imprint of Simon & Schuster, Inc.
1230 Avenue of the Americas
New York, NY 10020

First Gallery Books trade paperback edition October 2019

GALLERY BOOKS and colophon are registered trademarks
of Simon & Schuster, Inc.

For information about special discounts for bulk purchases,
please contact Simon & Schuster Special Sales at 1-866-506-1949
or business@simonandschuster.com.

The Simon & Schuster Speakers Bureau can bring authors
to your live event. For more information or to book an event,
contact the Simon & Schuster Speakers Bureau at 1-866-248-3049
or visit our website at www.simonspeakers.com.

Illustrations by Melody Hansen

Manufactured in the United States of America

10 9 8 7 6 5 4 3 2

Library of Congress Cataloging-in-Publication Data is available.

ISBN 978-1-9821-2125-9
ISBN 978-1-9821-2126-6 (ebook)

to the tired souls searching for home—
may you find it somewhere within these pages

contents

contents

contents

the bathroom (self-image and introspection)

contents

contents

foreword

A week before my eighteenth birthday, I vividly remember sitting on the floor of my mother's washroom, the words tripping off my tongue. I had asked for her permission to get my very first tattoo. "*Homesick*. I want it done in my handwriting. Right here," I said, pointing at the space along the bend of my left arm. I had penned a journal entry earlier that month in full detail about what being homesick felt like, and something about it felt closer to me than anything I'd ever written in the past. Having parents who divorced each other on two separate occasions, moving out of my childhood home where I'd spent seventeen years of my life, and desiring to attach myself to anyone who reciprocated with some form of affection, *home* was something that felt within arm's reach—yet also so painfully intangible.

Madisen Kuhn's stunning collection of poetry has an endearing way of reminding you that no matter how achingly distant the notion of home might feel, it's a lot closer than you think. Knowing she spent most of her adolescence looking for comfort in temporary places makes you feel less alone and more reassured. Growing up, especially as a teenage girl, it's easy to convince yourself that all the odds are stacked against you, and I marvel at how genuine Madisen puts those sentiments into words. You know that bittersweet feeling you get when listening to "Ribs" by Lorde while driving back home late at night? From the first poem in *Almost Home* to the very last, my heart filled with that same familiar nostalgic intensity.

To me this book is a gentle kiss on the forehead, a warm hug from an older sister, and a recognition that all beautiful things come from life's uncanny imperfections. It's an ode to celebrating the love you find within yourself, accepting the pain you spend so much time trying to suppress, and finding a way to turn that pain into something worth living for.

And in the mantra I know best: you will be reminded that you are your own home.

xo,
Orion Carloto

Almost Home

the kitchen

homeless

i raised myself to be someone who has no roots at all. i did it
to myself by never staying put, always jumping from place to
place instead of embracing one home. i have no home at all.
i am always wandering, always temporary, never knowing
how long each stay will last. and i cannot grow as quickly as
others when i am pruned. others who have steady sunlight
and familiar soil. they have real friends, and a permanent
family, and the coffee shop down the street that is always
there. i have train tickets, and parking tickets, and parents
who take turns making me cry, and google maps to help me
navigate short-term return address cities. instead of feeling
free, as wandering implies, i feel so incredibly trapped—
locked out of a safe space that everyone else spent their
adolescence building. mine was built on highways between
broken homes. i look at the photos they share and wish
someone had taught me how to swim with the tide. i began
drifting before i knew what it meant.

repressed

if you are
like me
when you
were young
you were
taught that
tongues
should sleep
safely inside
filtered mouths
not dressed
in honesty
or pleasure
but rather
in delusion
in carefully
memorized
scripts

when
your bones
grow around
these limits
they break
a little
with every
breath
they form
in twisted

patterns
through
knotted
childhoods
into
corrupt
adulthoods
where
we must learn
what it
means to
unravel it all

i am tired

my blood feels thin
within my veins
i've never been inside a home
that smells like freshly baked muffins
and acceptance and truth
my walls have always
been made up of bone and grit
the paint peeling from
overhearing so many lies
i'm not sure the voices even notice
the tone of carelessness
that lines their mouths
or that i have spent years trying
to unlearn their brokenness
the toxins that leave
a waxy film over
everything
i am

subjective

i do not feel compassion
for the man who made me
learn what it means to survive
to come out the other side
with wounds that hide under
repressed skin, only to reveal themselves
as silence or black ice caught in
a flash of remembering
i do not wonder what made him this way
think, did his mother hug him enough
when i hear his voice echoing
in nightmares where i cannot scream
and my legs feel like lead
burdened by the weight of all this baggage
a torn-up suitcase
filled with bloodred bricks—
it does not meet the carry-on weight limit
and i cannot unpack it

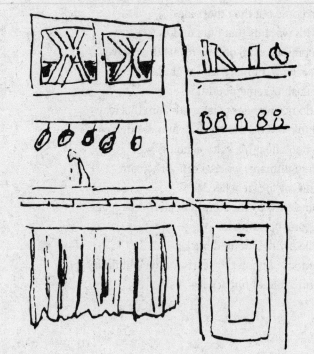

where do i go from here

there are ladybugs crawling all over my mother's house
or maybe it's my stepfather's house
or my brother and sister's house
it's someone's house, it's not mine
the ladybugs are scaling the windowpanes
polka-dotted carcasses line the kitchen floor
the faucet is dripping
it has been for years

you dream of growing up in a house with
a fireplace in the living room
you forget that you might live there
with people who won't fix it
instead, they grow cold
they throw cardboard boxes over the side of the front porch
and pungent trash bags into a rusting and dented trunk
the basement is unfinished, filled with dead mice
and pieces of my childhood that are easy to forget
the washer trembles when it's off balance
it won't stop till you rearrange the tangled sheets
there's a yard full of untrodden grass

it looks so large and whole from the outside

but there are holes in the walls
the size of doorknobs and fists

i would really like to go home

crying through space and time

i feel close to myself
when i cry
when my shoulders shake
it feels familiar
and safe

i am nineteen again
crying on the train
going home after
kissing a boy who
couldn't make me feel
safe

i am sixteen again
crying in my aunt's basement
thinking that out of all the
temporary beds i've slept in
this one is the softest

i am twelve again
crying with
the door closed
listening to the familiar bellows
of a broken home

when i cry
i am the same person
i have always been
it is like i am saying to myself

i'm still here
i'm still here.

blooming in concrete

the bits of apple
between my crooked bottom teeth
remind me of all the homes i've lived in
or almost lived in
that have left a sweet but spoiled taste in my mouth
as they rot just under my nose
i have yet to find a place to rest my head
not a clean pillow or warm chest would welcome my cheek
but i have looked and obsessed and tried
i have tried
my fingers ache from all the golden knobs i've reached out to
just to have them slammed in the door
again and again and again andagainandagainandagain
the wide and narrow roads are lined with
quaint front porches and crooked mailboxes
they are bursting with life
sad ones and dramatic ones and unremarkable ones
gasping and pulsing and humming
but there is nothing suited for me
all the welcome mats have been flipped over
before i clear the front step
so i keep running my tongue over the bite of longing
in places i'd rather not be

when i'm alone / in a coffee shop / i find myself

when i'm alone
in a coffee shop
i find myself
daydreaming about strangers
and mourning the life i want
but will never have

one with the steadiness
of a close-knit family
to wrap around me
when i cannot
keep myself warm

one with a father
who is brave enough
to face his depth

one with a mother
who does not settle
for self-preservation

one where they both
love me more than
they love themselves

vanilla

i hope you revel in the normalcy
when you feel the sunrise on your skin
walking down a brick path
on your way to class
i hope you breathe in the morning
hold the ordinary close to you
like a life that almost didn't happen

because for some of us
it didn't happen

i have never felt the blissful repetition
of being surrounded by what is expected
standing in seasons and looking at skylines
that your mothers and fathers
have stood in and looked at
mothers and fathers who do your laundry
when you come home to a home
that has smelled the same
for the past twenty years

so i hope that you laugh and drink
a little too much
and kiss people who make you feel seen
i hope you listen to bad music
and hug your friends too tightly
and skip your eight a.m. just because
you need slowness and stillness
and a coffee from the corner

almost home

and a breath of fresh air
in the morning
on a brick path
with the midday sun
on your skin

i would give anything to be you

estranged

i started letting the phone
go to voicemail
when i realized that
my father could exist
in the confines of my reality.
on my terms. in my world
that is painted in shy first kisses
under the boring light
of a november moon

where girls love girls
and boys love boys
and theys love thems

and no one stumbles
through hatred dressed up as tradition
or religion or opinions
without consequences.

before, i would shiver
at the sound of him
speaking confidently
of misquoted bible verses
and made-up statistics
that only serve as excuses
to remain unaffected
by the pain that others endure.

but now
my voice does not crack.
it does not quiver.
i know what love is.
i know that condemnation
comes from a lack of understanding.
a lack of trying to understand.

i don't believe in god anymore.

not the god i used to fear
under turquoise sheets
praying with small hands
that i wouldn't end up in flames.

not the god i held on to
while i hid the cuts on my thighs
from my friends at church camp
as i fed them lies, not because
i thought they wouldn't understand
but because i didn't understand
why the god-shaped hole
in my heart was filled,
but still
i was empty.

but i believe that jesus
doesn't like my father's politics
doesn't like that
he praises me in public
but dismisses me in private.

i know that he believes
maybe even prays
that my little world
will come crumbling down
and i will need him again.

but my world is not little. it is boundless.
it is made up of dreamers
and warriors and deviants.
it is a world where
i am not afraid to fall down.
i am on the ground.
i am looking up at the sky.
i am stretching out into life
where we peel back the skin
and reveal our tangled veins
and revel in the deep red
where everyone looks the same.

a world where
he does not get to make me feel
like a sinner or a stupid girl
or a disappointment

when for the first time
in my life

i feel like sunlight.

like i'm finally
getting it right.

to be announced

your parents
have wounds
they kept hidden
while pushing you
on the swing

now you're seventeen
squeezing your eyes
shut and daydreaming
about all the ways
you will be better

you can create an ocean
they cannot sail through
and put yourself
on the other side
once you've collected
enough freedom
to dig the pit
(it is reminiscent
of the one in your stomach)

the bridges
are yours to build
you don't have to be an island
but you don't have to be
public sands walked upon without care either

their wounds are
not an excuse to hurt you
they do not get
to point to theirs
while brandishing
dirty fingernails to
draw blood

but while their teeth
are sharp and their
eyes are dark
their broken skin
and blue veins show
there's still a
heart in there
somewhere

and maybe when i'm older
i'll be brave enough
to reach out
and feel it beat

aching in tandem

it is easy to cry
when you
slice your hand
on a sharp edge;
when the villain
is dressed in black
and leaves you alone
to bleed
on an empty street.

but what if the
injury isn't so sudden
what if
it blisters over time
a shoulder
freckled and burned by
an unintended fire,
lined with rocks
that used to sit
in your faded denim
pockets.

it feels impossible to bandage
the hurt that
is not a clean cut.
the wound that
is not
one-sided.

THINGS ARE SUPPOSED TO GROW HERE
IN THIS PLACE THAT
I DESPERATELY WANT TO CALL HOME

thin lines

there is a dead plant on the windowsill
brown and dry
like leaves on the sidewalk
of my favorite season
but things are supposed to live here
inside this place that
i desperately want to call home
(it doesn't feel quite like home, yet)

this place is meant to be
green and wet
and growing with hope towards
the sunlight
not disintegrating because
no matter how much i want
it to be filled with
beautiful plants
i never water them

there should be picture frames
hanging on the walls
but they're white with doubt
because no matter how much
i love the high ceilings
no matter how much
i love the man whose clothes
hang in the closet next to mine
i am afraid of the uncertainty
the fickleness of things

and quietly tell myself
that at any moment
i should be ready
to pack it all up
and go

paths

do you ever rewind
and wonder what
would have happened
had you stayed
in that small town
had you loved that one boy
had you never loved the other
are you really you or
is there some other
almost version of you
that is the real, real you
floating out there
somewhere
wondering why
you didn't choose
her

untangle

i don't think my mother
ever brushed my hair.
and if she did,
i can't remember it.
i could lie and say
that i wonder why,
but i know why.
it was because
she was busy with
my sister's brand-new curls,
busy tending to her own
dark roots and dry ends.

when i am a mother,
i will balance my sons
and daughters on my lap
and one by one
comb through
their soft mops
with patient hands.

they will never wonder
why i left them
to sort out
the knots
on their own.

they will know
i am there
to help untangle
the predestined messes
caused by the wind,
and caused by me.

deep down

there are some things
that are easier to write about.

like the vagueness of everything.
the self-hatred. the fear.
the shallow reactions.
the numbness of depression.
the clarity that comes with
a swift blow to the stomach.
the floating specks of light
you see before you hit the ground.

i know all the words
to these familiar poems.
i can trace them from memory
with my eyes closed.
i braid their hair every evening
and tuck them into bed beside me
where we dream about
our self-pity and
idealized happy endings.

but there are still dark figures
dancing in the shadows
of each day that i somehow
make it through,
impulsively pushed down
whenever they rise
up in my chest.

like the idea that things
can be grey and undefinable.
not wrong. not right.
just a blend of the two.

like how i feel about my mother.
shifting her in my heart
from a source of comfort
to a source of sorrow.
wanting her to be my rescuer
but also wanting to rescue her.
wrapped up in a tired box
of both total love
and quiet resentment.

like how i feel about my father.
words i cannot even fathom,
lost somewhere among
the razor-edged cracks
he left on the surface
of a child trying so hard
to be grown-up.

after a while,
you can trick yourself
into thinking you have said
all there is to say.
that there is nothing
left to write about.

but there always is.

there are those hazy shapes
lingering in your peripheral vision
begging to be set free

when instead, you decide
to write about the sky
or the sadness of winter
or a beautiful autumn day
again, again, and again.

prism

when i was sixteen
i would
wait in my room
all day
for the world
around me
to fade
for the eggshell walls
to crack and blend
into the bluish-white clouds

all i could see
were the whites
of things

the bleakness, the emptiness

i am a little older now
a little less sad

i walk my dogs in the evening
and smile to myself
about the pastel sunset
as it lowers itself
behind dark blue mountains

sometimes i call my mom
and we fill up the space
between us
with laughter about days
that did not feel funny
at the time

and when the walls around me
begin to feel
a little too bare
i hang up a piece of art—
a painting by klimt
a sentimental photograph
or something
a friend has made

anything
i can find
with a little color
to tinge the
vague and puzzling
task of existing

mistakes

sometimes
the unknown
shimmers
with beauty
unexpectedly
and makes you
question
ever trying to
stick to some
premeditated path.

i inhale breath
that never would've been taken
into lungs formed by chance
apart from the luck
of some wrong turn.
a left exit into a life
that was not planned.

often i gather bricks
that look like pillows
and fake prudence
to keep the walls
of oblivion up.

and yet

my father was not
my mother's soul mate.

but here i am.

if i could go back in time
and speak to some
twenty-seven-year-old stranger
i would persuade her
to keep looking. to be brave.

but then
there would have been
no poetry.

there would have been
no me.

i suppose someday
i will find the courage
to not fear
my own humanness.

what i was born from.
what i will inevitably make.
what will hopefully
turn out beautiful.

dream homes

some knobs come without locks
they live in houses where
the windows and doors are open
through every hour of the day
bees and flower petals
float through the open air
the cat comes and goes as it pleases

even when the seasons change
when the weather brings a gentle snow
and all the floors are covered in white
remember the beauty
of living without deadbolts
of walking into old spaces whenever
the sky reminds you by virtue of
clouds that look like a familiar face

you do not need to pack it all up in boxes
to mop the floor, to sell the couch
you can keep the door open
as long
as you like

family

i will make my own someday.
surround it with a white picket fence.
my children will write their own stories
with stronger bindings than mine.
i will do everything i can to make sure
the pages won't fall out, but if they do,
my babies will know where to go
to glue them back in.
i will stop wasting energy
on wishing it were different for me
and put all my love into
making it different for them.

the attic

my old self

i was alone in new york city
three stories up
between thin white walls
with cold tile
under cold feet
when i found my old self
in an old building
in an old city
once again

i found her
mapping out new wounds
on purposefully forgotten thighs
like she did
when she was a teenager
trapped in a room
of razor blades and unreality

i saw her in the mirror
wearing mascara
in smudged creases under her eyes
and she looked like a ghost
like the terrified reflection of someone
who had just been
thrust into burning light
after being buried for centuries
walked upon and
unremembered

i hardly recognized myself.
my old self.
i asked her why
she had come back for me

why
    now,
why
    here

she told me

she had never left.

when i wake

my head is void of muses
but plenty full of madness

i cannot give
the day in front of me
the attention it deserves
when my eyes roll back
into a cobwebbed skull
crowded with spiders spinning
worry out of ordinary things

i am so blinded by
my feelings of inadequacy
and the unavoidable
blankness of the unknown
that the world feels like
it's closing in with
all its noise and
unpredictability

in the morning
when i wake
the first thing i see
is the inside of my eyelids
too afraid to open up

i can feel the electricity
of anxiety
pulling the covers
off my naked body
crawling up my neck
and sticking its fingers
down my throat

so i roll over
and hug my knees
until i fall back asleep
hoping that when
i wake the next time
the sun will be
too bright to snub

the slightest bit lonely

why do i crumble
fall into pieces of
oats and sugar
something beautiful
in a white bowl, but
a mess on the floor

when i wake up
in an empty house
why do i wither like
brown leaves
under both brand-new
and borrowed boots atop
autumn sidewalks

when i'm alone
i'm alone
i'm alone
it is not enough
to eat breakfast
however small
to wash my hair with
coconut milk
to not step out into
the busy street

i freeze before the ice
touches me
i do not allow
the chance to warm
my own hands
i lie down on
dirty sheets
and wait for someone
anyone
anything
to awaken me

yellow

everything is covered in piss
i step in it, i sleep in it
i feel it running down my back
in the lukewarm shower
my slippers are sopping wet
right eye is red and stinging

it feels like nothing is uncontaminated

there are no black lights
i cannot find every stain to
kneel in front of with paper towels
and blot until my elbows ache
so i mop the entire floor
and throw away the couch

i was never told it gets so hard to feel clean

the shape of lonely

there is a girl
in a room
behind a door
with a knob
facing backward
so that the lock
is looking out
into the hallway
where anyone
can walk by
and decide
how long
she will stay
inside

i hate you, please hold me

when my eyes glaze over with
all the love i've never seen
all the biting words, all the biting silence
all the men who never tried
i am afraid of what it means
when your fingers get caught in tangled knots
as you run them through my soul

i have always been soft
when i should've been hard
and hard when i should've been soft

while i sit on the porch
with my wounds wide open
stinging and blistering in the heat
i wish you would just hold me
because i don't want to talk
about the hurt i've met
or the hurt i've introduced
because of it—
i know it's not fair
to scream and then ask you
to love me
despite me

the brutal line

sitting across from you
at the white kitchen table
or cross-legged on my side of the bed
is someone hollow.
not as sweet as a fig. not as dead
as the inside of a black rotting trunk
but close. i do not hold beautiful things
like a terra-cotta vase. inside my head
is a seam ripper that splits everything
down the middle. sometimes
you are standing in front of the bright window,
glowing like a saint. sometimes
i let you fall into an algae-lined pool
that i will not pay to have cleaned.
everything is floating within me.
i haven't figured out
how to anchor this stuff down.

no one ever taught me how.

i am grateful you are not me

i am grateful there is only
one of me
inside
this brain
this body
this film of consciousness
that stretches itself across
the pink mush
and cartilage
caught up in all the chaos
of thinking
and feeling—
at least you don't
live here too

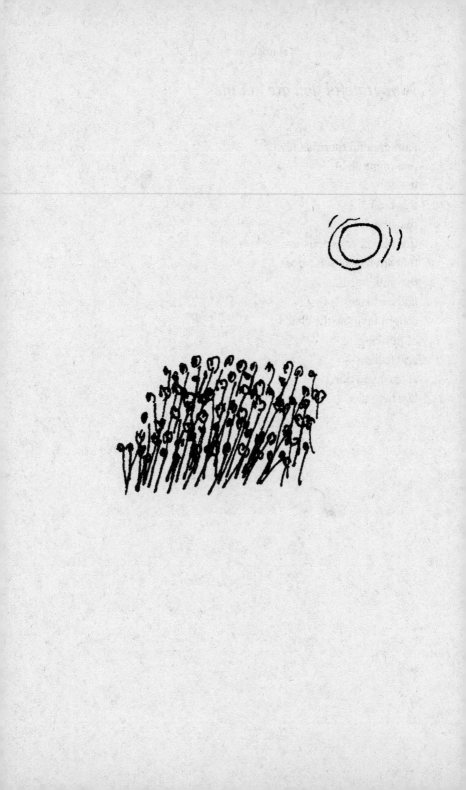

middle ground

i am
jumping
from edge to edge

the pale yellow edge
that looks out over
a field of daffodils
swaying in the wind
where people sing
and flow in the sunlight
with dirt beneath
their fingernails
and an abundance of
breath in their lungs

the dark grey edge
that looks out over
nothing

i cannot find
the place
in between

outage

in late january
when
the cold lingers
freezing and
refreezing
layers of cracked
ice
it feels like winter
has always
and
will
always
be here

the wind blows
so
heavily
in my heart
that
the power
goes
out

i can't keep the lights on

i can't keep the warmth in

my anxiety keeps me warm

the windshield
was blurred with
fog and rain
when you asked me
if i was cold
sitting there
next to you
i looked up
and said
i hadn't noticed
the icicles
hanging from the
bare tree branches
i was busy
obsessing over
the feeling
of my heart
skipping
inside my chest
and the burning
in my stomach
and the fear that
i would never
learn how
to be fully there
with you

too soon

it doesn't make any sense to me
that some lines just run out of ink
before getting to the good part

slip

when did the world
start closing in?
how did it happen
so fast?
and why do i believe
that it can't be
undone
just as quickly?

real things

some days i feel like sobbing
because i cannot believe
this life is real
that i get to experience it
firsthand
other days i feel nothing
i hide myself away
and try to recall
what it is like
to smell wildflowers
and float through
a moment without
remembering everything
that is at war
inside of me

a kind of amnesia

keep me awake
i keep falling asleep

i keep forgetting
that i have crawled
into places filled
to the brim with
heartbeats and
suffocating heat
just to find myself
with dry palms
and a soft jaw
minutes later

i hold my tongue
only to cut it off
i hate the feeling of it
inside my mouth
and i leave it for
him to hold
all pink and slimy
and frantic and cruel
and wonder
why it's hard for him
to read my poetry

and every night
i lay my head
against the chest
of indifference
and swear that
i can hear the
lazy thump of
his affection
resting shallowly
below thin ribs

i am kept awake
through the
loneliness hours
considering
my own
self-inflicted
wounds
instead of dressing
the deep cut
we both share

how it feels to panic in ordinary places

i live in front of a green screen.
the trees that line the streets
vary in shades of comfort, but
i stay the same inside
my rosso corsa ferrari.
ten minutes somewhere is
ten minutes anywhere. but
somehow one hurts more than the other.
when i am driving to the coffee shop
on the corner near
the dairy queen i used to go to
after middle school plays
the air smells like bonfires and
people who chitchat in the checkout line.
when i am driving on the other side of town
where the road is six lanes wide instead of two
the traffic lights sway uncertainly and
the air smells like shards of glass.
but nothing is different. the screen is still green.
the car is still red. the world is still open.
i am still the one behind the wheel.

madisen kuhn

grounded

there are some places
i cannot walk, so i must fly.

when i was little,
i loved the airport more than
anywhere in the world.
i was enamored of the lofty ceilings
and polished concrete floors
and all the people i didn't know
crammed in between.

but that was before
i had to grow up
and travel alone.
before i became someone
who is afraid of flying.

and despite my fear
every time i am up in the air
no matter how panicked
or trapped i feel
in those unchanging vinyl seats
when i look out the window
and see the miniature cars
passing slowly below me
i am reminded of the magic
of existing.

i feel small
in the best kind of way.

and when i land
instead of leaving all my
wonder and acceptance
among the bubblegum clouds,
i will carry it down with me.
pick it up along with my luggage
at the baggage claim.
pull it out of my pastel-pink suitcase
whenever i get hung up on my hurt
and remind myself
that you are just as small as me.

you are trying your best.

panic/overcome

life is too
fleeting
and beautiful
to hide away in
a green overgrowth
of escapism

the unease is temporary
the shaking
will wash away
like golden pollen
on a neglected windshield
in the warm bath of
an april storm

the impulse
of avoidance
persists
always outstaying
its welcome

but when faced
the panic
will melt away
in the bliss of
sunlight

so give in
to the freedom
of what is fated

the dread is worse
than the nightmare itself

because nightmares
end

but fear keeps us
half-awake

waiting for the monsters
to come out from
under the bed

we don't realize that
finally meeting them

could put an end to the
lies of a tired mind wandering

could change
everything

for the better

THE ABRUPT SPIKES
OF MY UPS AND DOWNS
LOOK LIKE THICK ICICLES
BARELY HANGING ON
TO THE ROOF OF A HOUSE
THAT WAS NEVER MEANT
TO BE A HOME

melt

the abrupt spikes
of my ups and downs
look like thick icicles
barely hanging on
to the roof of a house
that was never meant
to be a home

and i have to believe

that i will
stop holding
my hand
over my face
to keep the morning
out of my eyes

that i will
let go of
the familiar aching
of coldness
and let warmth in

that i will
find the light
instead of waiting for it
to find me

on a distant horizon
i can see myself
soaking in the brightness
as it melts my sharp edges

i will seep
into the ground
surrounded by
flowers and bugs
and lovely things
that are buzzing with life
welcomed into the place
where i was always
meant to be

the gradual onset of okayness

it feels like pulling fabric out of drawers
and none of it fits
last night, you put everything in the dryer
and fell asleep while
the things you thought you knew
tumbled and knotted and turned into
clothes that no longer fit

it feels like a bumblebee landing on your shoulder
you're supposed to stay still
until it realizes you are not a flower
and moves on
but it doesn't
it stays and buzzes in your ear until
you turn to dust or learn to scream

but then, one day
it'll feel like waking up to
rays of sun filtering through the window
when you haven't slept in weeks

like forgotten pocket change
like a present on your half-birthday
like a warm afternoon in the middle of january

and it'll feel like
it was always there—
you'd just forgotten
to turn the light on

the bedroom

st. christopher

i have forgotten to linger
in love with you
wanting only
to be found worthy
of your affection
revere your touch as holy
like goosebumps
in the italian sun
to write melodies
and ballads
and captions
not of purity, not of beauty
but of how you make me feel
forget all the rest
all the fighting
all the ugly
all the words
we didn't mean
for i am ill
when you are not around
and it is poetic enough
that you are broken
yet you are
what makes me whole

werewolf

the familiarity of a body
that is not your own
warms the soft part of your hands
with all the
buzzing atoms and heart-jumps
that you read about
when you were young
in thick, quickly worn books
beneath your ugly duvet
by the light of your flip-phone

love felt miles and miles away
when you held
those sun chip and
chapstick-stained pages
of a vampire romance novel
inside your desk
while a teacher droned on and on
about things that felt
much less important

but here it is now
this love
that burns your tongue
but soothes you all the same
this love
that keeps you on your toes
and in the palm of its hand

almost home

this love
that turns over for you
to rub its back to sleep

and it feels like a dream
to fall asleep next to
this body
this tenderness
with skin like a furnace
that lights up
every inch
of your being

the little things

a small, fading hickey on my left breast
reminds me that you're the best
and that you love me
even when i'm picking at my face
in front of a dirty bathroom mirror
topless and unshowered

you're the best
even when you're the worst
even when you scream and criticize and roll your eyes
you are trying and you're human and
you see me

you're the best
because you care enough
to grab my hand and hold it
when you see that i'm digging my fingernail
into the side of my thumb

you're the best
you leave marks on my chest
because i told you that i liked it once
forever ago

undying

as he held me in his lap
with the window wide open
the white peeling sill
framing green old trees swaying
in the late summer dampness
the air holding the same steam
as it has since the beginning of time
i realized it has always been this way
our skin has never been sterile
there are a billion footprints in the sand
switch out the vessel
the souls will look the same
i am not the first to love
or be loved
or write about obsession
and loss
and movement
a thousand dead poets know
the weight of my heart
they have tasted the universe
in the mouths of their muses
assembled verses about goosebumps
that look just like mine
i am not afraid of the ordinary
of saying what has been said before
i feel safer knowing
i am not the first to ever feel this way
and i feel at peace knowing
i will not be the last

vows

i will wait up for you
i will kiss you at the front door
i will rub your back until you fall asleep
we will walk down tree-lined streets
in cities that are new to me and old to you
we will hold hands on trains, in museums
for years, until there are permanent tan lines
on our fragile, well-lived knuckles
we will find rest in one another
on long days, on slow days
together, you and i

what brings me peace

sun squares on the hardwood
the morning robins
and you.

still dreamy

i love a man who doesn't
read books or like coffee
but he wants to hear
every thought in my head
even the ones that i think
are too deep dark and ridiculous
and he doesn't really like poetry
but he likes mine
and he loves me

he is not the perfect person
i pieced together in the confines
of a teenage girl's brain

we won't fall asleep to infomercials
because he turns the lights out at ten
and needs the room to be pitch-black
so that he can close his eyes and fight
the fear of unconscious existence

and i won't walk into our
perfectly decorated kitchen
to see him reading the paper
in the morning
because we live in my mother's house
and he reads reddit on his phone
and is gone for work before i wake up

he is not at all what i pictured
but when i look forward
to all the life in front of me
i can't picture it
without him

magnetic

i used to think
we were painfully different.
polar opposites. north and south.
so different, we once believed
it could never work.
but maybe we're just
north and south poles
of the same spinning globe.
arctic and antarctic.
different but the same.

sometimes you feel so far away
but if i could just
get a little closer
i would see that we are both
made of the same stuff.
the same ice and snow and
heartbreak and healing.

i hope that when i start
to drift
like summer glaciers
in the southern ocean,
you will pull me back.

almost home

i hope that when the horizon
begins to blur into
black-and-white apparitions
i will immerse myself
in the freezing waters
and find the strength
to show you warmth.

i hope that i will keep
reminding myself—
in the dead of winter
in the peak of summer
in the moments
when all i can see
are the bright contrasts
—that you and i are more alike
than we are different.

the likeness of him

every day
i look into
a mirror
with smudges
all over the middle
framed in gold
with carvings of
birds and vines
at the edges
there are little cracks
that sometimes
my fingers
get caught on
and i bleed quietly
onto the cold
floor

it doesn't like
to be kissed
when my hair
is half up and
half down
but still
i leave my
balmy lip stains
defiantly on
the spaces
i can reach
and focus on

almost home

everything
in front of me
except for my
own
reflection

mojave

i love you but
i don't know how to be with you
when you take me to the desert
and fill my shoes with sand
i do not know how to keep moving
how is it possible that you can see everything
every cactus every rattlesnake
every drop of water that i've missed
and for me there are only empty dunes
sometimes i believe you
the mirages are real
i can reach out and touch them
but other times i am so afraid
that we are lost somewhere
in a damp dense forest
and i just cannot see
the color green

the difference

you and i
are two people
who would like
to fade from the earth
knowing that we cared
and tried
and did
all that we could
to be better

but some days
usually the days
when you wake up
at six in the morning
and i hit snooze
until ten
i am stuck
feeling mismatched
and broken

like someone who will
always be watching the sunrise

describing in great detail
its orange and pink brilliance
the way it warms my freckled face
as the windshield thaws
in late december
while others
vanish into the skyline
encompassed by light
and envied by me

the greatest difference
i can grasp
between our
ambitions of growth
is that
i am always saying
one day
and you are always saying
today.

romanticizing the unromantic

late at night
i sometimes think that
if i were alone
like i always used to be
i'd be drinking hot tea right now
and watching television in bed
without headphones

after midnight
maybe with the lights on
i'd stretch across
two halves of a bed
that aren't really halves
without two bodies
and write poetry
about how
i'd give anything
to fall asleep
next to you

what else is there

i feel so restless
and afraid that
another universe exists
where kissing feels
different

where lips are soft
and eager
where mine
are red and swollen
from all the attention

but i will never know

because i've only ever
kissed you
and you don't really like
kissing me

what it feels like sometimes

it is a
pitifully poetic idea
to write about
someone
who doesn't
like poetry
and will never read
these pages filled
with words
about him.
what i wouldn't give
to read poems
written about me.
even the ugly ones.
maybe when
i am long gone,
he will finally
pick up
one of my books,
when i am
not there
to beg for his
attention.
but then
it will be too late
because
it's already
too late.

almost home

i am lying next
to him,
but i am
somewhere else.

one fantasy

sometimes i drift
into another life
where ivy crawls up
the side of
a white brick building
to my left
as i walk
hand in hand
with you,
your parents
strolling slowly
a few paces behind.
everything is still
inside of me.
i do not fear
the future
nor ache for
the past.
my heart beats
quietly next
to yours.
i am only here,
only there.
i do not drift.
i listen to love songs
and am reminded
of my own
happiness.

two souls

after two souls have mixed
like sugar and salt
it takes a seasoned tongue
to discern which grains
are salty
which are sweet—
which notes came from you
and what tastes
like them

is it possible to ever
sieve out a soul mate
from the sand on the shore
of your essence

or are you left with a mouthful
of uncertainty

sadness that bites like
a sour lemon

left with gaps that feel hollow

can you ever get them back

chameleon

i always knew
we would say our
goodbyes
before the night
faded out
but knowing that
did not keep me
from wrapping my
love around you
the way bright green ivy
wraps itself around
a white brick château
in the south of france

with
one last kiss
on the cheek
a knowing gaze
and a solemn lip
i will tell you

it has been
a privilege
to know you

an ode to almost lovers

in this life
you and i
are like
helicopter seeds
spiraling down
from the same sycamore tree
caught in
the same wind
but destined
for different
pieces of earth
and although
we'll grow
apart completely
i hope to see
your orange
maple leaves
as large as
the palm of god
scattered across
a crooked sidewalk
on a warm
autumn evening
when the sky
has just begun
to fade
and i
have just begun

DO YOU EVER WONDER
WHAT THE MOON IS THINKING?

the moon

i do not speak your name
i cannot even whisper it
instead, i hide it in my dreams
under my sheets
beneath a sky that sees all
but does not burn my skin
do you ever wonder
what the moon is thinking
does she gaze down solemnly and see
a fading opus
or a symphony simply tightening its strings
for the final act
do you think it makes her sad
to see the greens replaced
with soot and plaster
the seas rising to meet her
with an apocalyptic kiss
the falling tide
the slow recession
reminds me that
she keeps our secrets
but i think it breaks her heart

intimacy

touch me
any way you know how
through your words
or your subtleties
with your art, your silence
and i will flip through books
and think of you
i will see you in the space
above upper lips
i will feel your hands on me
when you are not around
and you will hold me
with quiet intensity
without arms or expectations
when no one else
is looking

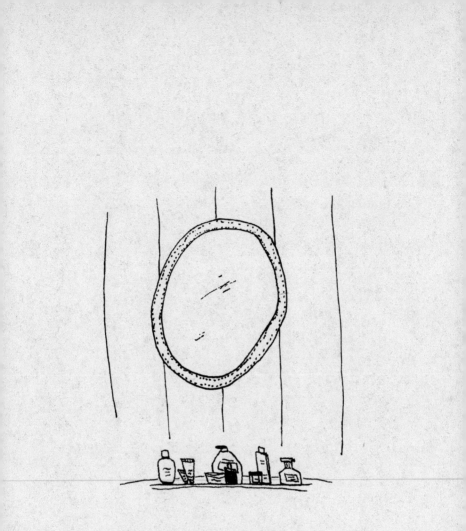

the bathroom

impostor syndrome

does your skin ever melt into the mirror
do your palms ever reach the other side
will these reflections ever make sense
ever feel familiar
ever seem right
whole
on purpose

do you find yourself, one day
staring back, composed with a straight spine
thinking, *i know her well*
able to plaster her on billboards and
not shiver with questioned identity

i used to feel sure of who i was
when i was sixteen
there was no alternative
to knowing and
naïvely believing that
i would always feel certain

but now
i can't decide
what answer to give
when asked the question
who are you,
really?

and i am terrified
i'll never look like the person
i hope to see
when i squeeze my eyes shut

how should i define these smudged edges

if i am not
the things
i think and feel

(because sometimes
i think and feel
awful things
that i know
aren't true)

and if i am not
the things i do

(there are
a lot of things
that i would like to do
that i simply don't
like play piano.
and read more.
and be kinder. braver.
more alive.)

then what am i?

am i the wanting?

the reflection that i see
in my head
but not in the mirror?

or am i
the person
standing
in front of you?
all flushed
and slight and
callow

how do you see me?

do you
see me
at all?

caelum

in another life
i wear clay beneath my fingernails
and linen pants around my hips
fastened with a braided leather belt
rescued from my mother's closet
one she wore in the eighties
when she met my father on the seaside of france
i carry flowers from the corner
down a gum-stained sidewalk
past the park i fell asleep in during one
slow sunday afternoon
there are cherry-red stains on my pillow
some from my lips, some not
i've never been in love
but i've never felt alone
my nose is slender
and my collarbones flaunt themselves
beneath tanned skin
i am someone who drinks vodka and
orange juice while watering my plants
a long-haired cat licks its paws
in the windowsill
as i lie naked in the sunlight
reading tolstoy and kerouac
and obscure poetry introduced
by the neighbor next door
none of it matters
i am just like a cloud
like a creaking step

i share myself only through
spearmint breath and coffee dates
here are my sweaty palms
here are my uneven bangs
you will never know me

---

brooklyn baby

i could be that girl
whose voice is low and melodic
and coats your mouth with
acacia honey
whose eyes are the color
and depth of
midnight
whose presence is thick like
new york summers
rosy like
los angeles in early spring
if i braid flowers in my hair
if i write enough poems
if i learn to show the skin of my essence
but remain an abyss

i will stop making art
when i become it

i do what i'm supposed to

right now would be a great time to write poetry

it's past midnight, everyone is asleep
there is a pale blue light coming from the hall bathroom
my thoughts are lingering in distant, buried places
recalling nightmares as dreams
drawing halos over the heads of humans

but i don't want to

i am tired
and bored
and afraid my words will smell like stale clichés

maybe i can just dip my toes in reflective black holes
feel the coolness, the deadness
the other world i'm too afraid to fall into
like quicksand or riptides or working nine to five
maybe i can lean in, just enough, to get a glimpse
of what i do not want

i promise i don't think of you.

baby teeth

when i think about
all the lives i've lived
in twenty-two and a half
short years
it both breaks
my heart
and gives it
enough breath
to keep floating
forward
into a life
that is waiting for me—
to prove to
my younger self
that better days
were always
fatefully
prophetically
glistening just beyond
the silhouette
of longing

multitudes

i am so many different people.
i am vibrating
with all the lives
i have lived.
i cannot make out a face
in the perpetually spinning
chaotic blur that pulses beneath
this translucent alien skin
stretched across these bones.
these bones
that have broken
and healed
into different patterns.
these limbs
that feel heavy
and delicate
at the same time.
there are too many
stories existing inside me.
i don't know how
to tell you
just one of them.

hiding. being found.

i am hiding in the coffee shop
in the post office parking lot
i am hiding in the music playing
through the car speakers and
in the pages of my journal
i am looking out at nothing
i am fading under the dust
and i can feel myself falling
asleep at the wheel
i can sense the moments
on my tongue like tasteless ghosts
but when i pull over
and take a long look
at the hands in my lap
i don't know
if i'm trying to hide myself from you
because i want to be
less of me
or if i'm trying
to find myself
in the places you are not

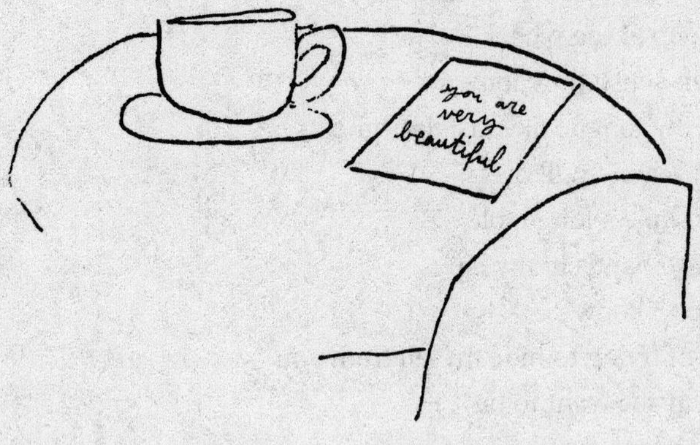
you are
very
beautiful

sad girl energy

a man handed me
a note today
at the coffee shop
that said
in careful cursive
you are very
beautiful
and i laughed
and my face turned
very red
and i didn't
believe it
not even for
a second

float away

sometimes
i bump into the thought
that i don't really care
about anything

not school
not being pretty
or healthy, or better.

when you wipe off
the good girl cosplay
the soft peach blush
and the freckles
and the lip gloss

the straight a's
and the sweet potatoes
and the self-discipline

you will find a wild thing
dancing around
in her underwear
drinking iced coffee
for lunch and
doing nothing but
writing and reading
and abandoning any
semblance of sanity

completely consumed
by all the things
i shouldn't be.

and when i have
destroyed everything
around me
with my negligence
and delusion

when the decent ones
have seen themselves out

when there is nothing
left inside of me

there will always be poetry.

madisen kuhn

cold hands hold no expectations

there are edges of loneliness
that are soft
these are the edges that i think about
when i feel suffocated
by the pressure of being more than i am
or less than i am
or really anything but me
for someone else

protection

i wake up with flushed cheeks
sunburned by
white sheets
and forbidden dreams
splotchy with weariness
but lacking warmth
the pinkness doesn't paint
a portrait of youthfulness
a portrayal of life
nothing so tender
although i wish it were
(i wish i was tender, soft, silky
lovely like a statue made of marble)

when i stare at my reflection
in a mirror covered with peppermint toothpaste
rubbing lavender ice cubes
across my red face
it only reminds me of
how it feels to lie out somewhere
for too long; to fall asleep under
an unassuming sky
and wake up
to the painful reminder
that i have forgotten
to put sunscreen on

i wish i could find
any simple way
to flip life over
to the cool side
of the pillow

i would like to be remembered as
someone who never gave up

i wonder why / there is so much buzzing inside of me / all
the time / i would like to be remembered as someone who
never gave up / so / if my mind never gives up / if it is always
buzzing / if that won't change / maybe i can change the
sound / the frequency / maybe i can switch the tracks on my
train of thoughts / teach them to soothe / instead of sting

purpose

the world
is spinning
and it has
nothing
to do
with me

self-talk

it's difficult
to know if
i'm thinking
of myself
too little
or too much
—too little
and all the dishes
are washed
all the clothes
are folded and
put away
but the room
becomes dark
and i have
forgotten
to eat.
—too much
and i become
stuck inside.
far away.
you wouldn't
like
the sound
of the voice
inside
my head.
—so it must be
in the thinking

itself.
i must be
doing it wrong
entirely. because
on both ends
i am collapsing.
perhaps
it is a question
of quality.
not quantity.
i shouldn't be
considering
how to think
more or less
but better.
just better.

french braids

i am not sure if my mother ever french-braided my hair when i was little.
if she did, it was before i was old enough to remember.
still, no one ever taught me.

i taught myself when i was fourteen how to braid my little sister's hair.
my heart would swell when i watched her eyes light up at her own reflection.
but i could never do the same for myself.
i tried, sporadically, but not long enough to find success.
by the end of each attempt, i'd angrily tear my fingers through
the disappointing braids. they never saw the light of day.

i stopped trying.

i am twenty-two now.
after a shower, i twist my hair into a wet messy bun
where it dries into a knotted representation of my self-doubt.
i hold my chin in my hand while i gaze at girls with tight braids
and colossal smiles that melt away the jealous parts of me
leaving only a wiry frame of indulgent self-pity.

it is easy to feel bad for myself.
to daydream about childhoods that looked nothing like mine.

but i know it is not too late.

i could be the girl with french braids.

i could hold my elbows up over my ears in front of the mirror
every day until they shake from exhaustion.
i could unravel them every night and crawl into bed with soft waves.
i could fall asleep without wishing i were someone else.

if only i understood that i do not need anyone to hold my hand.
to braid my hair for me. to wipe away my unproductive tears.
to tell me that i am more than enough.

impossibilities

i want a better life
and i have the power
to create it.

even if it feels impossible.
plenty of things have felt impossible
but ended up becoming
a part of me, my story
a tale i tell
with a wide grin.

all the impossibilities
are interwoven into
every part of my being.

falling in and out of love.
moving in and out of cities.
coming into and out of myself.

i am forgetfully
and beautifully
composed of
all the things
i thought
i could never do.

I CAN SEE THE SILHOUETTE
OF WHO I WOULD LIKE TO BE.

thirties

i have paid the fines
of dozens of unopened
overdue library books.
i love curling up
in a big leather armchair
while the sun reaches out
to me through the window
as time slows
and my coffee grows cold.
but tolstoy and fitzgerald
sit on my shelves
or in my purse
carried everywhere
and collecting dust.
i can see the silhouette
of who i would like to be.
the curve of her hip
the stillness of her limbs.
she grows her own herbs
and tries out new recipes
while her husband is at work.
she doesn't mind driving
for hours alone
and enjoys singing
along to the radio
going five under the speed limit.
she is not in a hurry.
she is proud
and sure

and poised.
she reads books and returns
them on time.
she gave up on dreaming
and hoping
and longing
a long time ago
and finally
decided to start
living.

soft

one day, i woke up
and there wasn't any uncertainty
to wipe out of sleepy, half-open eyes

i pulled on a green sweater over silky underwear
my collarbones and teardrop breasts
hidden beneath the comfort of thick clothes
where the wind could not reach me
where the lingering eyes of old men
with wives and wicked grins
could not make themselves at home

but still, i glowed with all the allure
that i feel in small skirts and thin tops
that hug my delicate edges on warmer days

in mom jeans, and no makeup, and dirty sneakers
i felt like orchid petals still growing on the stem
like the lipstick-kissed brim of a porcelain teacup
like the skin of ripe persimmons just picked from the garden
like the matte dust jacket of a brand-new book
like kitten paws stretching after a long nap
like the curved back of a marble sculpture
like pink icing on a homemade birthday cake

how to love

love poems
about other people
seem to write themselves.
they get plastered up
on billboards and screamed
out of open sunroofs.
but self-love poems
write themselves quietly,
like a child tiptoeing
to the kitchen for
a midnight snack,
afraid to wake even the dog.
it's like catching my reflection
in a store window and
just barely smiling
so no one else will see
and get the chance
to accuse me of vanity.

and when all the worthwhile
things i am not, and the
painfully broken things i am,
are glaring back at me in
every shiny spoon and
public restroom mirror,
it feels like detangling
a necklace to get one bit
of confidence straightened
out inside of me.

i could write love poems
about every cloaked stranger
on a crowded sidewalk
who glances in my direction,
but it has taken blue moons
another person saying it first
and years of weekly therapy
to figure out how to write
something beautiful
about me.

the garden

something beautiful

me.

open ends

i realize
i am not the only one with questions
and that my questions
do not make me naïve, or messy,
or void of poetry

there is no such thing as
finished or whole

when things seem to harmonize
on the outside
is it a true reflection of inner peace
of the honest-to-god self
or has she just learned
by paying close attention
how to appear intact

even the poets who
speak in absolutes and preach
lovely words of conviction
still question the purpose
of all these words
written for me and for you
and for all the leaves
on trees with numbered days
who cannot read

almost home

there is not enough time
nor is it worth yours
to memorize
all of the answers

I HOLD ON to
THE WAY THE AIR FEELS IN OCTOBER
IT BRINGS OUT THE BEST IN ME

the tenderness of autumn

i hold on to
the way the air feels in october
it brings out the best in me
unlike the violating heat
of august that fills the space between
the dirt and the heavens
only a handful of moons prior to
the golden treetops and the
ritualistic pumpkin and maple
that stir our hearts and reveal
our need for stupid, cheery things

the earth is falling asleep
laying its head to rest
in the fading foliage on the ground
folding up the day into smaller
and smaller glimpses of light
but here i am
bathing in the soft wind
here i am
grinning in a grey sweater
here i am
waking up

center of the universe

i want to drink
chai lattes at nine
in the evening
and stay up till dawn
dancing on
the soft carpet
of my living room
with records
spinning and crackling
and candles
burning and crackling
and us
swooning and crackling
as the pale yellow light
of a new day
creeps in through
the swaying blinds

i fall asleep to wake up

i nap for my art
i curl up on plush couches
my small dog leaning on
the soft part of my stomach
the drapes drawn, the lights on
it's the middle of the day
there is nothing better to do (surely)
all morning i bounced my leg
bit my nails, pretended to focus
on the things right in front of me
—but now,
as i squeeze my eyelids shut tightly,
as to not let in any brightness
or glimmer of productivity,
the stifled muses float to the surface
glistening like light specks
across a dark lake
and when i wake
i write poetry
about all the ideas in my head
in the spaces between dreams and reality
that are too romantic
too absurd, too childish
to pay attention to
during the responsible rituals
of everyday life

warmth

there is not one
there are billions
they dance in the sky
beside clouds and light
while you stare at your feet
the ceiling
your hands
you will not find it there
(in the spaces void of feeling)
you will find it alone in the grocery store
in your best friend's living room
in the eyes of someone new
the person staring back at you
in the foggy bathroom mirror
she knows of love's abundance
like the stars in the night sky
worn in tangled hair
it will never leave her

the first day of spring

the first day of spring
this year was
in early february

the first day of openness
after a winter of
staying closed

it was the first day
that i walked outside
and didn't need a coat
to protect me
from the sharp air

it was the first day
that i breathed in existence
and didn't feel the need
to protect myself
from the world

my dog is my role model

in the middle of the day
after a long nap in the sun
my dog sifts through his
woven basket of toys
until he finds his favorite one
and almost every time, after
plenty of spinning and tossing and chasing,
he flips the tied rope over his head
so that it hangs around his neck
like a noose

entirely unaware
of what it looks like
he continues to play
jumping up on his hind legs
and chasing his tail
completely amused with
himself and the huge world
that holds him up

eventually he wiggles his way out
leaving the plaything somewhere
for me to pick up
and put away

almost home

and when he trots back
to his little square of warmth
on the hardwood floor
where he sunbathes
until it's time for dinner
i kiss him on top
of his soft and tiny head
feeling silly
for how envious i am
of a dog—

of his ability
to be so blissfully unaware
so trusting
of the world
around him

lovely

i am jealous
of what you have
but not
of who you are

regardless
it withers me

so instead of watching
your garden grow
even if i find it
utterly dull

perhaps
i should start digging up
the earth in my own
neglected plot

and observe
what becomes

unprovoked

on one overcast afternoon
under a dull sky
when the wet grass tells a story
of a storm you just missed
i will learn to compose my heartbeats
to match the slow
dripping of water
off a steel roof's edge
i will play its strings like a harp
the soft music will regulate
an even pattern of breath
a rising chest
falling
there are no bruises
i do not wince
i've forgotten the feeling of
sharp venom
my blood pumps the antidote
and the ire at my temples
in my lungs
on my chest
dissolves into a vapor of knowing
i am safe
within myself
no matter how low the clouds hang

philadelphia in may (a daydream)

this morning, the rain halfheartedly falls.
puddles collect on the gleaming blacktop.
i am in my blue and worn overalls
on the covered stoop, sucking a cough drop.

my apartment is in center city.
there are not many trees, but the ones that
bloom in spring look like wild cotton candy.
their petals get brought inside by the cat.

sometimes i feel like i'm suffocating
so i open the windows to let in
a breeze. not today. today, i'm waiting
outside with goosebumps all over my skin.

so that when the sun decides to wake for
summer, i will be the first to greet her.

orion

if you look up, you will see
the bright-eyed and
the widemouthed—
the interesting, the casual, the adored
glistening in the warm night
peered at through microscopes and
telescopes and stethoscopes
far and far away

we are desperate
to be close
close and close and
close enough to see the blemishes
the scarring and the peeling
effaced by obvious and biased inner commentary
they're just not as red or sore as mine
perhaps they were formed under
a different kind of sun

what does the unfamiliar heart say
does it sound at all like mine
will i ever escape the sloppy grasp of dullness
will the world ever swallow me whole
if i count the days on both hands
on toes, on eyelashes—
if i only eat green things and
read tattered books and
pretend that i don't mind—will i ever

break the mirror
will i find seven years of good luck
between the jagged edges

to exist as a reflection
is to not exist at all

there are lonely, dark purple heavens
waiting for you to sever your longing gaze
to stop lying to yourself
and begin living somewhere beyond the moon—
to realize, with closed eyes
you belong to the sky

the birds

i thought i missed
los angeles
because every morning
i would sit in my apartment
and listen to the birds sing
and the cars pass and
small snippets of songs
blaring from strangers' stereos
it was warm there
and the streets were lined with
beautiful flowers and cactuses
and i was very sad there
i was full of fear and pain
deep gashes i let bleed
in the comfort of
isolated days
that turned into weeks
and, tragically, months
but when i look back
i don't think of that
i think of the birds
and how i wish
my apartment in virginia
had birds that sang to me
through the window
and then this morning
i sat in the grey chair
in the corner of the room
that i rarely sit in

and closed my eyes for a bit
and i was still, and i listened
to the purring world around me
i heard the dishwasher running
and cars passing in the distance
and then i noticed
the birds
and my heart laughed at me
because i finally realized
i'd just been living
too far
from the window

write it all down

i keep falling asleep
with poems on my mind
something about
my mother
something about
missed connections
i repeat the idea in my head
try to make it stick
enticing them to get
caught in my psyche
like flies in honey
i swear i won't forget
but when i wake up
the window is open
the screen is intact
the little bugs are sweetly
humming on the outside
too wild and busy
to whisper what was felt
the night before

all of the beauty i am ready to be

there is a modest
one-story home
with white stucco walls
and a red tiled roof
waiting for me somewhere
near a floridian beach.

the yard is flat and dry.
some days, i'll lie there
on top of a patterned quilt
in a two-piece,
hand cupped over my forehead,
reading a thick memoir
that is on loan from
the library that sits on
the other side of the brush,
beyond the wooden fence.

winter will just be a memory.
every week, my toenails
will sink into the sand
wearing a different shade of pink.
i will not fold away
my sundresses and shove them
under the bed.
they will only leave
their wooden hangers
to be worn and washed.

time simply records the falling
and growing and falling of things.
one of these days,
i will be the budding lily
pushing up through dirt
to greet the other side with
all of the beauty
i am ready to be.

i have fallen enough.

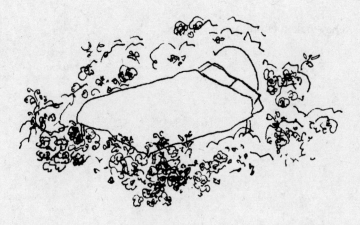

regardless

even when
it feels impossible
to hold herself up
on two uncertain feet
and she finds herself
impaled on the sharp
twists and turns
of existing—
the birds still sing
on their fragile branches
in their white pine trees
every morning
dressed in a hopeful
shade of peach. and once
she has cried and screamed
and tried enough
for one weary day—
her bed is there
like the promise
of sunrise
waiting to hold her
until the night
has passed

when in doubt, look up

the sky gave me a hug
this evening
by cloaking itself
in my favorite shade
of lavender blue
at sunset
and i hugged it back
with a smile
and a poem
and the greatest sense
of gratitude

the world is a beautiful place

the world is a beautiful place
where lives can overlap
at just the right time.

every now and then,
we get to rope off
certain connections
in our memories,
leaving out the realities
that would undoubtedly tarnish
the shining gold place
they hold in our hearts.

grandparents. almost lovers.
weeklong friends
from summer camp.

perhaps time
is more romantic
than we think.

perhaps she puts us
in just the right place
to love some people
without interference.

don't waste them

the mornings you roll over
to lean against a warm chest.
the hickeys that make you blush
but do not keep you from
putting up your hair.
the quietness that invites you
to find yourself within.
the books that remind you
what it means to feel alive.
the afternoons spent writing in cafés
losing track of time between the cursive.
the slow dancing on bamboo floors
naked and humming and laughing.
the life that is flashing before your eyes.
all of it. all of it. all of it. all of it.
the memories you will hold on to
when you have forgotten
everything else.

gratitude

the rain has stopped
and the birds are lining
the sidewalks, shaking
their feathers dry.
today will be slow
and i'm okay with that.
i'll cook and clean
and sit on the balcony
and breathe in the mild air.
i am happy and lucky
to be here.
it makes my heart heavy
to know that i must
remind myself of that
so often.

the front porch

what happens next

the unknown
is a shapeless and
daunting thing
i try not to get
too close to it
because i'm afraid
i'll walk into the dark
and never see the light
again
if i go there, i'll leave
the world
with just a memory
of me
but if i stay inside
this cage of
passive survival
far away from
what i have yet
to see and feel
and fall
in love with
there will be
no memory of me
worth leaving
behind
anyway
so
i suppose
we will

figure it out
eventually
how to surmount
this black hole
this blank space
i promise you and
i promise myself
we will figure it out
maybe not wholly
but enough to make it from
this moment
to the next

when i kept going

i kept anticipating
blocked-off entrances and
handwritten out-of-order signs
over gas station bathroom doors
rusting at the corners

because each time i got in my car
(which smells like wet dog
and lavender)
i found a reason to turn around
i convinced myself that
the green lights were not meant for me
only back roads and passenger seats

the sun was not there
when i kept going
the sky was full of grey
and i could feel the rain in my chest
i didn't need it to be a perfect summer day
i just needed to believe
that i had enough light within me
to make it through

give yourself a break

you are young. you are just beginning. you are not supposed
to be complete yet. now is when you lend out your heart to
be broken, and then learn how to mend it. now is when you
make mistakes and discover who the fuck you want to be
and how you want to live. there are no rules. only the ones
you write. and there are people who will love a version of
you that doesn't even exist yet. there are memories to be had
that will become stories that you tell in a rocking chair on
the front porch of your final hours. and there are lessons you
will sit through with a grimace but pass on with a smile. let
yourself breathe. let yourself break. let yourself piece things
back together. you are alive. forever changing. still growing.

it's not too late

even if
you decide at
the last second
to choose
happiness
(to choose life)
that is enough

follow that glimpse
of clarity
straight into the sun

chase down
the chance
to expand, to exist
among the beams of light
and unexpected bliss

jump into
the subway car
that will carry you
to the version of you
that glows and spins
with hands
reaching heavenward
before it pulls away

courage that
lasts a second
leads to
a world filled
with joy
and excitement
and inner peace
you didn't believe
existed

old oak tree

i shouldn't expect
to stand still
while the untethered
and unbothered
wind demonstrates
the power of the universe
as it sends the rain sideways
twisting dead and
soon to be dead leaves
in its playful vortices

my roots
are brand-new
my limbs are still
thin and delicate like
soft green saplings

for a while
i will bend
and shake
and fear
the thunder
until i dig down
deep enough
in the dirt

madisen kuhn

the bending
and the shaking
is part of
the beauty of growing

if i stay here long enough
if i let the storm soak into me
instead of letting myself
run for cover
i will become
strong and steady
like an old oak tree

i will wear my growth rings
like gold medals—
proudly parading
the proof of
what i have weathered
—there will be
too many to count

and i will find myself
smiling at the sky
when the dark clouds roll in
because i am
still here
still standing
after all this time

one million paths all lead back to you

there is no right
there is only left
and sideways
and upside down

and in every direction, there is something
something to hold on to
to get lost in
to break you into something new

there are not just two roads that diverge into
either cracked dirt or soft grass

every path
is made up of mirrors
and all they ask
is that
you keep your eyes
open

july will be better than june

one day
it will be easy to breathe
my lungs will inhale flowers
and honey
it will be second nature
like riding a bicycle
like tying a shoe
like swallowing a pill
and i will hold on
tightly
with shaking hands
until then

i hope you live (a letter to my future self)

i hope you have bruises.
i hope there are calluses on your palms.
i hope your feet are tired.
i hope you fail.
i hope you sometimes hurt.
and i hope you feel the overwhelming joy
of going on
in spite of it all.

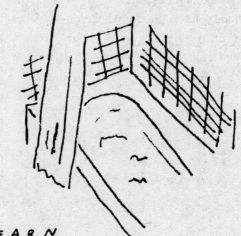

LEARN
TO FLOAT

embrace

we are taught by the rain

the soft water
the heavy tears

a mother who runs a bath without asking
she just knows

trench coats are worn only if you care
about getting wet

when you swim at the beach in a storm
you do not know the difference
between the sky and the sea

learn
to float

to catch the droplets
on your tongue

to run naked through puddles
forget your galoshes at home

and then
you will understand

constant reminders

there are some things
that never change
like the way
the sky looks at night
after it has snowed
all faint
and yellow
and familiar

even when your parents
got divorced
the sky still looked this way

even when you spent
an entire week in bed
it snowed the next month
and the sky lit up in the evening
like dim fireflies
hiding behind wispy clouds

even when you're twenty
-something
and you've just
been hit with the
heavy awareness
that everything
is up to you

it will begin to flurry
and you will look up
and realize
the sky is always
there to remind you
that there are small
unchanging things
like this
that we can hold on to
whenever the winter
feels unbearable

slow down

when it arises
as it inevitably will
roll the idea
the feeling
that grips
your neck
over your tongue
like a gumdrop
instead
of immediately
swallowing it
whole—
there are worlds
inside of you
that turn
bit by bit
on their
leisurely axes.
let your breath
mimic those
light atmospheres
their
forgiving
gravitational
pulls.
teach your
heart to float
more often
than it sinks.

significance

when you stick your eye into the mouth
of a telescope
sometimes all you can see is the moon
it is obvious and bright and easy
but the stars are there
there are billions of them
burning their effervescence into the sky
and here you are
floating in between the stretches
of night and explosion
held up by the universe

you are stronger than you know

awareness

i hope you make time
to be lonely

—not the kind
of lonely
that rings in your ears
and causes the room
to close in
like a cruel hand
gripping the most
vulnerable edges
of you

—but this. the kind
of lonely
that forges a path
of clarity
where the sound
of rushing water
beside the trail
you walk on
with tired feet
every day
suddenly sounds
like a symphony
of realization

do not fear
the quiet moments
the milky spaces
in between;
reach out to them
—the gentle wind
the rays of sun—
with soft hands

let your love
and beauty
and childlike wonder
expand
in the moments
that are quiet enough
to hear
your resilient heart beat

to love is to live

just as the sun rises without fail
even when the world feels like it's ending
like it couldn't possibly still be filled
with light

one day, it'll hurt less
it'll feel more like a good memory
and less like
being stuck in a bad dream

and it's impossible to understand why bad things happen
how they could possibly be turned into good
but you'll doggy-ear pages
and write down notes in your phone
notes that look like prayers but sound like hope
and you'll smile and smile and smile
and smile and smile and smile
because to ache is to have known love

and to love
is to live
without regret

madisen kuhn

the cost of things

the thought that
one moment
could've changed
everything
makes my throat sting
makes my chest
feel heavy with
longing

but i cannot
change the past
—it is so far away

perhaps the warped
and broken
pathways are
what i owe the stars
what i must endure
to write what
i have written
and to know
what i have
known

my hope is that
you get to skip
these sketchy alleys
that i have
mapped out
for us

and maybe
soon
i will come across
another moment
the kind that
changes everything
(they are everywhere
all the time
i promise you)
and i will
choose differently
this time

please don't settle

do not settle
for a love
that doesn't
ignite you
but more importantly
perhaps
more important
than anything else
i could say—
do not settle
for a you
that is less than
what you want
what you know
you are meant
to be

random. lucky.

it all changes so quickly
you have to keep your head up
and float, soft belly to the sky
mirror the clouds
with your light and airiness
let the deep blue and ancient
rushing water of the river
gush and slow as it may
you are just a lucky coincidence
a feather on the surface of the world
watching the days unfold
and trying to find meaning in the creases
but let it go, let it go
wrap it around you and
be glad that you don't have to wonder
what it feels like to be alive

so it goes

if i looked at everything in front of me
the way i look at everything behind me

(the subtle joys. the ignorant bliss.
simpler. always simpler.)

i would have everything
i've always wanted.

i would stop worrying whether
i'm doing this right.
if tomorrow will be better.

if i could just see it all right now,
i could hold the tender life i ache for
in the soft palm of my hand.

because when it snows,
i hide inside and wish for summer.
and in the summer,
i hide inside and wish for snow.

always pining
for the next season where
i will still be tearing forward.
always forward.

but every book i've ever read
tells me that
these days are not meant to be
skipped through.

everything i want
is already right here
in the soft palm of my hand.

i don't hate february anymore

february only feels cruel
because we expect it to be
something it's not.
the days linger now
and we've tasted the memory
of spring,
wishing for the sunlight
to hold more warmth
than it does.
we forget that it still snows
this time of year.
we loathe the storms
we longed for in december
and pack away
our winter parkas
on the first barely warm day.
but february is not meant to be
march or april or may
it is meant to be
exactly what it is—
the in-between place
that keeps us from
getting lost in extremes.

i hope you know that
there are februarys
for everything.

you are home

you wait for it to come
that aching feeling
that sinking feeling

like waking up
before running a marathon
you didn't train for
like all the ocean is
in your lungs

but then you take a breath
another one, another one
until all of the sky is
in your lungs

and after a very, very
long winter
of bitter snow and
frostbitten toes

the sun hits you
just barely
just enough to turn
your skin a shade
of gold

and everything
is okay

afterword

when i think about all the places i've lived, i realize it's no surprise that i have struggled with defining "home." i have never possessed a sense of stability, emotional or otherwise. it has taken me a while to figure out that stability is not just based on external factors—where you live, your family, relationship status, or career—but is something that you cultivate within, so that wherever you go and whatever life throws your way, you are confident and secure in yourself.

i have spent a lot of my life finding my identity in my pain and unfortunate circumstances, and instead of unapologetically going after what i want (or even believing that i am capable of doing so), i have settled into the comfortable role of just feeling sorry for myself. feeling like a victim became familiar. so when faced with a difficult situation, my first instinct is not to come up with solutions, but to hide away; to find someone to comfort and validate me. i rarely have faith in my abilities to overcome anything.

but after years of avoidance and shrinking myself at the first sight of discomfort or adversity, i am tired. i am not who i would like to be. i am ready to stand up straight, shoulders back, and lean towards the hurdle. if i jump and miss, that's fine. i'll try again. because sitting on the sidelines, picking at the grass, and making dandelion crowns with my fear has not given me the life that i want.

i think the biggest aid in coming to this conclusion has been my attempt to fully understand myself. my first love, christopher, played a huge role in helping me see myself with a different pair of eyes. he encouraged me to dig deep, to go further than the initial thought or feeling, and to make sense of each harmed and harmful part of me. from the beginning of our relationship, i craved his pity. a big part of me wanted him to see me as a victim and to rescue me. for a long time, i resented him for not treating me that way, but now i can fully see and appreciate that if he had fed my desire to be consoled, i would've likely continued to see myself as a victim for a very long time. him seeing me as a strong, capable, and powerful person—when i could not see this in myself—is the greatest gift he could've ever given me.

understanding myself began with understanding my family and my formative years. i was raised as an only child until i was ten. my parents lived in different cities for most of my childhood. when i was eight, my parents officially divorced, but their relationship had been on-and-off since i was born. as a child and a teenager, i would alternate between favoring my mom and favoring my dad, depending on who was willing to give me the attention i desperately craved. with the clarity i have today, i accept that they are two imperfect people who are still carrying the pain caused by their parents, as i do my best to figure out the hurt i carry from mine. with all of their flaws and mistakes, i still love them, even when i do not like them. even when i hate them. even when they hurt me. i will always love my parents. but the truth is, neither of them cared for me the way i hope to care for my future children, should i ever become a mother. i carry a lot of pain that they passed on to me, and i'm doing my best to mend it now, so that i do not pass it on to anyone else.

growing up, i romanticized things that were standard in many of my friends' lives. i always wanted a dresser that was neatly organized and a bathroom drawer where my toothpaste and mascara would live without disturbance. instead, i had a half-unpacked suitcase always holding some uneven combination of clean and dirty laundry, and a toiletry bag that was never emptied. i daydreamed about having one house that i grew up in, that i could go back to and rest in whenever the world felt too large and overwhelming. but by the age of seventeen, i had lived in eighteen different homes. at twenty-three, the count is up to twenty-four.

i am beginning to recognize what it takes to feel at home within myself. in order to fathom who i am, and why i am this way, i must walk through each and every room of my heart—even, and especially, the ones where i'd rather keep the door shut tight and locked. i must accept that i am a product of my environment and my relationships. i am affected by everyone i have loved. and while there is pain, and scarring, and fear, and anger there—i can learn from my past. i can learn from my parents' mistakes and grow into something better. it's entirely up to me.

it takes acceptance. i did not have the childhood i wanted, and i do not have the perfect family, but i cannot spend my life wishing things were different. i am lucky to have what i have—my beautiful siblings, a mom who accepts me for who i am, and a hometown that i love. i refuse to spend the rest of my life feeling bad for myself and envying the upbringings that appear more intact than mine.

because we all carry pain. we all find ourselves gazing over at our neighbors' lawns from our beautiful front porches instead of tending to our own gardens. but there is peace and freedom in acceptance. there is joy and celebration in taking hold of your life, deciding what you want it to look like, and stopping at nothing to make it happen. i don't think it's easy. and i think being young is accepting that we don't have it figured out, but we don't really need to have it all together to feel at home in this world. we get to build it together—with all our imperfections and dreams and messy stories.

i think i'm almost there. i hope you are too.

acknowledgments

thank you to the baristas who made all the coffee i sipped while writing this collection.

thank you, melody hansen, for the stunning illustrations that perfectly capture the energy of this collection. i cannot believe i got to work with such a talented artist whom i've appreciated for a very long time. i knew years ago that i wanted you to illustrate my third book, so this was truly a dream come true.

thank you, orion carloto, for being a wonderful internet friend and constant source of inspiration. i will forever admire your well-rounded artistry. your foreword is the cherry on top of this collection.

thank you, christopher, for the support, love, and inspiration you supplied through the cold winter months. i am grateful for the way you believed in me, even (and especially) when i did not believe in myself.

thank you to my family—mom, natalie, jake, the greens, the ottavianis, the lovins, the wolfingtons, and anyone who has ever made me feel at home.

thank you to my dogs, kanye and fin, for keeping me company and providing comfort while i wrote the more difficult pieces in this collection.

thank you to my childhood dog, angel, for being my best friend for nearly thirteen years. we love you and will miss you forever.

acknowledgments

thank you to my agents, erin harris and katherine latshaw, for your guidance, wisdom, and encouragement.

thank you, molly gregory, my editor, for the invaluable insight you provided. i am beyond thrilled to have access to your brilliant understanding of literature. you have helped me bring my poetry to another level—this collection would not be what it is without you.

thank you, gallery books and simon & schuster, for continuing to bring my poetry to more and more readers. i am continually blown away by the doors that have been opened for me with your help.

thank you to my readers, my followers, my friends for being an overflowing spring of validation and kindness. i will never get over the love you have shown me. you will always have a home in my heart.